MICROSOFT COPILOT USER GUIDE

Unlocking the Potential of AI in Your Daily Tasks

BEN TAYLOR

TABLE OF CONTENTS

Here's a suggested table of contents for a Microsoft Copilot User Guide:

CHAPTER ONE

INTRODUCTION

Overview of Microsoft Copilot

Microsoft Copilot integrates an AI-driven ad-on in several microsoft apps that promises to run productivity and automatically to automatically run functions. Depending on highly advanced machine learning and natural language processing, Copilot helps users users to automate regular tasks, automate regular tasks and make data analysis accessible.

Key Features:

1. **Writing Assistance**:
    - Email, reports and other documents suggest real -time suggestions to draft, which enables users to get more clearly.

2. **Data Insights**:
   - Analysis explains data in Excel and other programs, produces summary, trends and visualizations, which simplifies the understanding of complex data.

3. **Task Automation**:
   - automatically makes regular tasks such as email management and file organizations in scheduling meetings, freeing users to focus on high-value activities.

4. **Integration with Microsoft 365**:
   - Originally works in Microsoft 365 apps (such as Word, Excel and Teams), provides a consistent user experience and enhances cooperation.

Integration with Microsoft 365

5. **Customizability**:
   - o Users are able to customize Copilot features according to their special requirements, modify the settings to personalize their workflows.

6. **Learning and Adaptation**:
   - o User learns from constant conversations, improves its suggestions and recommendations over time.

Microsoft Copilot intends to strengthen users by increasing its capabilities, facilitating daily tasks and ultimately conducting efficiency and innovation in organizations.

Key Features of Microsoft Copilot

1. **Intelligent Writing Assistance**:
   - o This tool provides immediate writing assistance through Microsoft applications such as material manufacturing tips and grammar and style improvement in Microsoft applications such as Word and Outlook.

2. **Data Analysis and Visualization**:
   - o Analyzes data sets in Excel, offering insights, creating charts, and generating summaries to help users make informed decisions quickly.

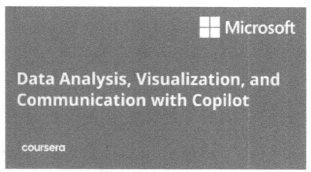

Data Analysis and Visualization

3. **Task Automation**:
   - o It performs regular function activities without schedule by schedule and sending email answers that accelerate the process.

4. **Contextual Suggestions**:
   - o This immediately suggests real time what you do to make the work more efficient.

5. **Seamless Integration**:
   - o Copilot Microsoft supports 365 tools so that users can easily switch between applications without losing their workflow speed.

6. **Collaborative Features**:
   - o Copilot lets users work together in teams and other apps to work together and share ideas and make their team projects effective.

7. **Customizable Experience**:
   - o Users can personalize the copillot through settings and preferences to meet their personal functioning requirements.

8. **Learning and Adaptation**:
   - o The equipment improves results by applying user data from previous activities to give better suggestions as the user interacts with it more.

9. **Security and Compliance**:
   - o The system follows strict security protocols at an enterprise level to protect confidential data while running AI functions.

Security and Compliance

These abilities are designed to help users improve their work, while making teamwork and task management easier throughout organizations.

CHAPTER TWO

GETTING STARTED

System Requirements for Microsoft Copilot

Users need two main things for Microsoft Copilot to function properly:

Hardware Requirements:

- **Processor**: 1.6 GHz or fast, double-core processor or higher.
- **RAM**: 4 GB RAM minimum (8 GB or more recommended).
- **Hard Disk Space**: At least 4 GB of available space.
- **Display**: Your system must show 1280 by 768 pixels or more in screen resolution to work optimally with Microsoft Copilot.
- **Graphics**: Microsoft Copilot needs a DirectX 10 compatible graphics card in your PC for proper operation.

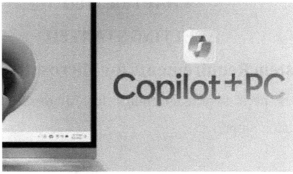

AI Hardware Requirements

Software Requirements:

- **Operating System**:
    - Windows 10 or later
    - macOS Mojave (10.14) or later
- **Microsoft 365 Subscription**: Users Need Microsoft 365 Membership and Microsoft Copilot Access to Complete Their Microsoft Facilities.
- **Internet Connection**: You need a reliable internet connection to use all Microsoft Copilot online updates and features.

Browser Requirements (for web applications):

- Microsoft edge, google chrome, or latest version of Safari

Additional Requirements:

- **Microsoft Applications**: The Microsoft Office applications such as Word, Excel, and PowerPoint require a compatible version to utilize Microsoft copilot effectively.

Your system must match these requirements to use Microsoft Copilot at its full potential.

Installation Guide for Microsoft Copilot

To start Microsoft Copilot follow this installation procedure:

Step 1: Check System Requirements

Verify that your device complies with essential hardware and software conditions for Microsoft Copilot.

Step 2: Subscribe to Microsoft 365

1. Go to Microsoft 365 website.
2. Select the subscription option that includes Microsoft copilot coverage.
3. Use the directions to begin your Microsoft Copilot sign up process.

Step 3: Install Microsoft Office Applications

1. **Download Microsoft Office**:

    o Go to Microsoft 365 portal (portal.office.com).

    o To start the installation process clicks the Install Office button and follows the presented steps for download.

2. **Run the Installer**:

    o Open the downloaded file and start the setup program with one double-click.

    o After starting the installation process you need to follow the instructions on the screen to finish the setup.

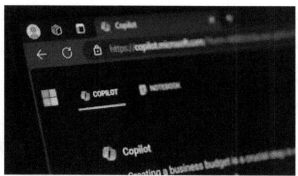

Install Microsoft Office Applications

Step 4: Enable Microsoft Copilot

1. Start any Microsoft 365 program (Using Words Excel or PowerPoint).

2. Log into your Microsoft 365 account if asked to continue.

3. Check for the Copilot option which normally appears as a menu button or icon inside the program.

4. Confirm that your program has received all recent updates since Copilot only shows when enabled:
   - Go to "File" > "Account" > "Update Options" > "Update Now."

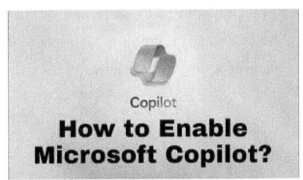

Enable Microsoft Copilot

Step 5: Customize Settings (Optional)

1. Find Copilot settings in the applications menu area.

2. Tailor Copilot settings according to your work habits with choices like picked language support, help mode selection and personal security controls.

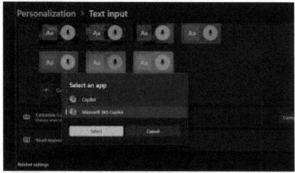

Customize Settings

Step 6: Start Using Microsoft Copilot

1. Inspect the different tools Microsoft Copilot offers.

2. Use Copilot to help you become more productive while creating texts and inspecting data plus running automatic procedures.

Start Using Microsoft Copilot

Troubleshooting

- Check your network connection and verify if your device matches all system needs when problems happen during setup.

- Visit Microsoft's support site for more guidance or dial their customer service number to receive assistance.

You can now start using Microsoft Copilot to increase your efficiency levels.

Setting Up Your Account for Microsoft Copilot

To access Microsoft Copilot you should configure your Microsoft 365 account. Start by following these basic steps to begin working with Microsoft Copilot:

Step 1: Create a Microsoft Account

1. **Visit the Microsoft 365 Website**:
   - Go to <u>Microsoft 365</u>.

2. **Choose a Subscription Plan**:
   - Go to "For Home" or "For Business" selection to view offered plans.

o Pick a Microsoft Copilot plan that belongs to your chosen subscription type.

Choose a Subscription Plan

3. **Sign Up**:

   o Click on "Buy Now" or "Try for Free."

   o After you click the "Create an Account" button follow the instructions to start your Microsoft account setup. Give both your email and set up a password during account creation. You have to provide any required information in the given fields.

Step 2: Verify Your Email Address

• Check your inbox from Microsoft to verify your account sign-up.

- Open the email to find the verification link then click it to confirm your Microsoft account.

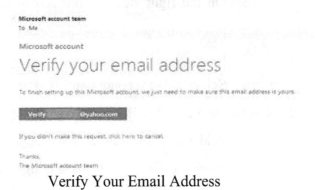

Verify Your Email Address

Step 3: Sign In to Your Microsoft 365 Account

1. **Go to the Microsoft 365 Portal**:
   o Visit portal.office.com.

2. **Sign In**:
   o Enter your Microsoft account email and password.
   o Follow any two-step verification process when asked.

Step 4: Set Up Your Profile

1. **Access Your Profile Settings**:
   - On the right side of your screen click your profile image or initials under the main menu.
   - Select "My Account" or "View Account."

2. **Complete Your Profile**:
   - Add your essential personal details into the available fields such as adding your name and security preferences.

3. **Adjust Privacy and Security Settings**:
   - Look through all privacy settings and modify them to match what you prefer.

Step 5: Install Microsoft 365 Applications

- Use the previous instructions to install and download Microsoft applications according to the provided setup guide.

Step 6: Launch Microsoft Applications

1. **Open an Installed Application**:
   - Start the Word Excel or PowerPoint application that belongs to Microsoft 365.

2. **Sign In**:
   - When asked to sign in click on the MS 365 account field and enter your Microsoft 365 account details.

Launch Microsoft Applications

Step 7: Access Microsoft Copilot

- Find and open the Copilot feature available from the Microsoft application interface arrows.

Access Microsoft Copilot

Tips

- Set your Microsoft account settings to work best with the platform and choose to get system alerts when new tools become available.
- Check for current updates in your programs so you can use new Microsoft Copilot features.

Feel free to use Microsoft Copilot right away!

CHAPTER THREE

USER INTERFACE OVERVIEW

Dashboard Layout of Microsoft Copilot

The Microsoft Copilot dashboard helps users work better by providing an easy-to-use display of all its system features. This section describes the major features of its design:

1. Navigation Menu

- **Location**: The navigation menu of Microsoft Copilot stands on the left side of your dashboard screen.
- **Features**: As part of the Microsoft Copilot dashboard users can easily select from their installed Microsoft applications and find essential account management settings.

2. Main Workspace

- **Description**: This space allows users to work directly with all their Microsoft document files.
- **Features**:
  - The main work area lets users create and update their work files in real time.

- The system presents relevant Copilot suggestions according to what you do in your current work.

3. Copilot Suggestions Panel

- **Location**: The software show suggestions mainly on the right panel or in floating boxes.
- **Features**:
  - Offers real-time suggestions for writing, data analysis, and task automation.
  - Users can use their mouse to select Copilot recommendations which automatically appear in their work.

4. Search Bar

- **Location**: At the top of the dashboard.
- **Features**:
  - Users can access documents templates and help resources through a direct search function.
  - Search bar helps users find Copilot functions and commands through its unified system.

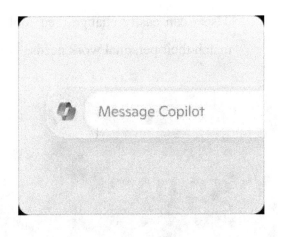

5. Notifications Area

- **Location**: Typically in the top right corner.
- **Features**:
  - Displays alerts for updates, new features, and collaborative comments.
  - Copilot lets users see what tasks and actions it takes.

6. Quick Access Toolbar

- **Location**: Usually above the main workspace.
- **Features**:
  - The toolbar gives users the ability to save, undo and redo often-used commands from its customized menu.

o   Users can easily change their tool setup to match their personal work needs.

Quick Access Toolbar

7. Profile and Settings Menu

- **Location**: In the top right corner.
- **Features**:
  - o   Users can view and change all account functions from this menu.
  - o   Users can choose to end their work session or switch between their different account entries.

Summary

The Microsoft Copilot dashboard uses clear navigation elements to help users find tools and features that improve their work performance. The system allows users to work efficiently while Copilot generates valuable advice.

Navigation Tips for Microsoft Copilot

When you know how to move around the Microsoft Copilot dashboard you can use this software to its fullest potential. Here are some helpful tips:

1. Familiarize Yourself with the Layout

- Spend two minutes examining the dashboard elements by studying the navigation menu and Copilot suggestions area plus the main workspace.
- Finding your workspace elements will help you work faster.

2. Utilize the Search Bar

- Look up documents and features through the top search bar.
- Enter your task keywords for Office results instead of using menu navigation.

3. Pin Frequently Used Tools

- Include your top commands on the Quick Access Toolbar by pinning them to the toolbar.
- Keeping frequently accessed items pinned to the toolbar makes them available at your fingertips.

4. Explore the Navigation Menu

- View different Microsoft applications including Word and Excel from the navigation menu on the left side. The menu lets you find and access your latest documents and template options to start work immediately.

5. Engage with the Copilot Suggestions Panel

- Leave your Copilot suggestions panel open to receive recommendations during your work process.
- Select suggestions from the panel to use them immediately in your work.

6. Keyboard Shortcuts

- Memorize and apply keyboard shortcuts that perform basic tasks such as saving documents (Ctrl + S) and undoing recent actions (Ctrl + Z).

- You will work faster thanks to the unique keyboard shortcuts.

7. Use Contextual Help

- Open the built-in application help to find out how to use a particular feature when needed.
- The system shows tips particular to your current project settings.

8. Collaborate in Real Time

- Share your work right away within Teams or Word collaboration tools to team up with colleagues instantly.
- Check if the software has tools that allow you to join group projects and view updates made by other members.

9. Keep Updated

- Check for updates often to receive the newest application functions and updates.
- Check your notifications regularly to discover new Microsoft features and product upgrades.

10. Feedback and Settings

- Tailor your settings to match how you want Microsoft to notify you while providing Copilot help.
- Contact Microsoft to report your problems and give product recommendations.

Adopting these tips will improve your interaction with Microsoft Copilot and boost your work efficiency.

CHAPTER FOUR

CORE FUNCTIONS

Writing Assistance in Microsoft Copilot

Microsoft Copilot includes tools that enhance your writing output and help you create better content. This section explains how Microsoft Copilot functions with detailed information for users:

1. Real-Time Suggestions

- **Contextual Corrections**: As you type Copilot suggests better ways to normalize verbalization punctuate and structure sentences.

- **Word Choice Enhancements**: Copilot suggests better words as you compose text to make your message easy to understand.

2. Content Generation

- **Drafting Assistance**: The tool makes text based on input you define when working on drafts of your documents. The system helps users produce documents like emails as well as reports and other documents in a fast manner.

- **Templates and Frameworks**: You can pick from many ready-made document templates that you can modify with Copilot.

3. Formatting and Structuring

- **Automatic Formatting**: The program formats documents automatically by adding headings bullets and numbered lists to make your text easier to follow.
- **Outline Creation**: It produces writing patterns based on your major points which lets you plan your structure first.

4. Style and Tone Adjustments

- **Tone Detection**: Through tone analysis Copilot identifies your writing style and recommends how you should adjust your tone for formal, informal, persuasive and informative approaches.
- **Consistency Checks**: The system checks for ongoing stylistic and verbalization consistency across your document.

5. Summarization and Paraphrasing

- **Content Summarization**: When you give a long text to Copilot it creates a short summary containing the most important points.

- **Paraphrasing Tools**: The tool helps you find better ways to express sentences when you want to normalize verbalization or normalize verbalization.

Summarization and Paraphrasing

6. Language Support

- **Multilingual Capabilities**: Copilot handles multiple languages through text translations and detects regional writing differences.

- **Language Learning**: The tool explains language rules and writing standards to help students who speak English as a second language.

Language Support

7. Integration with Collaboration Tools

- **Real-Time Collaboration**: In Word and Teams Copilot enables team members to edit documents and provide immediate feedback at the same time which boosts teamwork effectiveness.

- **Commenting and Feedback**: Team members can write feedback to documents which Copilot helps insert into their work.

Summary

The Microsoft Copilot writing tools help users manage their writing work and create best quality texts that organize information clearly and attract audiences. Microsoft Copilot helps you at all points during your writing work whether you need assistance with a short email or a complete report.

Data Analysis with Microsoft Copilot

Microsoft Copilot can read and explore different data sets rapidly to show users meaningful trends inside the data. This section explains what Microsoft Copilot does during data analysis tasks:

1. Automated Data Insights

- **Quick Summaries**: Copilot uses data sets to produce quick summaries that display important patterns and findings.
- **Highlighting Patterns**: Copilot uses data sets to produce quick summaries that display important patterns and findings.

2. Interactive Data Visualization

- **Chart and Graph Creation**: The system allows you to produce different visual displays such as charts and graphs directly from your data. The system detects which visualizations produce the most helpful results regarding your data.

- **Dynamic Dashboards**: Design dashboards that update their data in real time to provide instant access to performance tracking.

3. Data Cleaning and Preparation

- **Error Detection**: The system finds recent errors in data and suggests necessary changes to hold correct data formats.
- **Data Transformation**: It helps users make raw data workable through operations such as combining data groups, switching database views and adjusting data types.

4. Advanced Analysis Techniques

- **Statistical Analysis**: Through Copilot guidance you can run statistical methods such as regression tests with t-tests supported by calculations.
- **Predictive Analytics**: Built-in artificial intelligence systems predict future outcomes using past data performance.

5. Natural Language Queries

- **Ask Questions**: Users can enter regular language questions like "What happened to sales numbers during the last three months" and Copilot answers the query with data findings.

- **Interactive Reports**: You can make detailed data investigations by running custom reporting plans through the system.

6. Integration with Excel

- **Excel Functions**: Copilot works with Excel by suggesting features and functions plus handling data handling processes while keeping up with spreadsheet formatting.
- **Conditional Formatting**: Copilot applies automatic data format preferences that highlight trends directly in the results.

Integration with Excel

7. Collaboration and Sharing

- **Real-Time Collaboration**: Several users can work together with the team in real time to view data simultaneously.
- **Sharing Insights**: You can distribute visualizations and reports to your colleagues or partners at both company and external locations.

Summary

With Microsoft Copilot data analysis users can explore their information more effectively to improve decision making through valuable insight generation. Microsoft Copilot brings excellent value to users who work with numbers no matter their business focus area.

Task Automation with Microsoft Copilot

The automation system in Microsoft Copilot helps users cut down manual work to boost their efficiency and productivity. This section explains how to use Microsoft Copilot for task automation purposes:

1. Automating Repetitive Tasks

- **Routine Operations**: The system can perform everyday processes including data submission to prepare reports and email answers for enhanced efficiency.

- **Customizable Macros**: Microsoft Copilot permits you to generate and put into action macros inside Excel together with other applications to automate your workflow.

2. Scheduling and Reminders

- **Meeting Scheduling**: The system finds available times for all meeting participants and creates meetings that sync with their appointed calendars.
- **Task Reminders**: The system will send you notification alerts to help you plan your schedule properly.

3. Email Management

- **Smart Replies**: The framework makes context-based e-mail reactions through Savvy Answers to permit speedy fitting answers.
- **Email Sorting**: The framework sorts approaching emails by applying preset rules to set up legitimate organizational capacities in your inbox.

Email Management

4. Data Updates and Notifications

- **Dynamic Data Refresh**: Energetic Information Revive lets clients establish automatic information source upgrades to induce ceaselessly overhauled data without manual dealing with.
- **Alerts and Notifications**: The framework will give particular notices approximately information

changes that meet specific conditions such as when deals goals or stock amounts reach basic levels.

5. Integration with Microsoft 365 Apps

- **Workflow Automation**: Microsoft Control Computerize can work with Copilot to generate workflow computerization that permits distinctive Microsoft 365 apps to associate (such as mail connection programmed sparing to OneDrive).
- **Task Assignment**: The framework will naturally disperse assignments all through Microsoft Organizer when ventures fulfill their needs and time limitations.

Integration with Microsoft 365 Apps

6. Document Management

- **Version Control**: The framework ought to have built-in form control capabilities which empower programmed adaptation administration with current changes continuously protected.
- **Content Updates**: Report substance remains up to date naturally when information sources or connected records experience any alterations.

7. Custom Automation Solutions

- **Tailored Scripts**: The robotization instrument gives clients with two choices: the creation of custom scripts and the determination from existing formats for specific computerized strategies counting report creation or progressed information preparing.
- **AI-Powered Recommendations**: Microsoft Copilot analyzes client exercises to generate automated suggestions which recognize modern robotization conceivable outcomes through work designs and commonly executed errands.

Summary

The Microsoft Copilot mechanization framework erases schedule forms which empowers employees to concentrate on critical imaginative assignments. The mechanization highlights empower your organization to boost productivity and diminish blunders whereas upgrading efficiency levels.

CHAPTER FIVE

INTEGRATING COPILOT WITH OTHER APPLICATIONS

Microsoft 365 Integration with Copilot

Microsoft Copilot acts as an integrated ecosystem component of Microsoft 365 which provides better collaboration features and productivity improvement to every application. The integration between Copilot and Microsoft 365 comprises this description of their connection:

1. Cross-Application Functionality

- **Unified Experience**: The Copilot function delivers a uniform user interface experience that operating across Microsoft 365 main applications including Word, Excel, PowerPoint, Outlook and Teams.

- **Data Sharing**: Users can transmit information and analytical findings between applications automatically instead of manual movements which promotes more synchronized work environments.

2. Enhanced Collaboration in Teams

- **Real-Time Collaboration**: Users can leverage Copilot to perform real-time team work during document collaboration across Microsoft Teams platform on spreadsheets and presentations.

- **Meeting Insights**: The meeting summary function in Teams allows Copilot to generate condensed discussions and show significant to-dos while offering associated resources.

3. Integration with Outlook

- **Email Drafting**: Email Drafting through Copilot allows users to produce emails and respond to messages and condense lengthy email chains into organized summaries.
- **Calendar Management**: The system enables users to schedule events automatically and send professional invitations directly through their Outlook emails without leaving the platform.

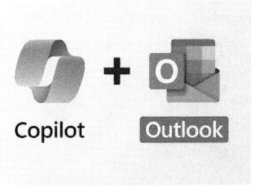

Integration with Outlook

4. Data Analysis in Excel

- **Smart Data Insights**: Smart Data Insights enables Excel users to access data analytical tools which create data visualizations as well as summaries and charts from existing data.

- **Natural Language Queries**: The system enables users to demand data inquiries through normal language requests which produce answers together with visual explanations.

5. Content Creation in Word

- **Writing Assistance**: Users can deploy Copilot's writing assistance feature for Word to get advice on document grammar along with style and tone enhancement as they prepare their documents.

- **Template Utilization**: The platform includes multiple document templates in a unified collection for users to produce professional content more efficiently.

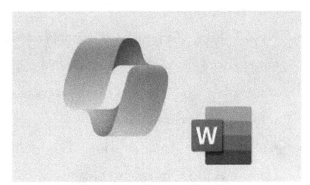
Content Creation in Word

6. PowerPoint Presentations

- **Slide Generation**: The system can automatically create presentation slides by processing Word text and Excel spreadsheet contents to maintain consistent content flow.

- **Design Recommendations**: The design recommendation feature of Copilot helps users improve their visual presentation design through constructive template suggestions.

7. OneNote Integration

- **Note-Taking Support**: The tool helps users automatically organize their OneNote notes with summaries to enable easier access in later information retrieval tasks.

- **Collaborative Note Sharing**: The system allows team members to share notes via collaborative platforms which creates shared organizational spaces for improved group input.

OneNote Integration

8. Security and Compliance

- **Enterprise-Level Security**: The security system of Microsoft 365 enables enterprise-level protection which ensures data protection during both collaboration activities and the automation process.

- **Compliance Management**: The system enables businesses to meet regulatory standards through its tools which support safe information sharing and permission-based access controls.

Summary

Microsoft Copilot when linked to Microsoft 365 delivers a robust platform which boosts work efficiency alongside teamwork operations along with data management functions. Users benefit from Copilot features when they work in their familiar Microsoft 365 environment because this combination streamlines workflows while improving task communication and output.

Third-Party App Connections with Microsoft Copilot

Microsoft Copilot gains additional functionality through its third-party application integration which helps users improve productivity while working between different software tools. The following information explains these connection methods:

1. Integration with Popular Apps

- **CRM Systems**: Users can access CRM platform data from applications like Salesforce and HubSpot through Microsoft applications and generate reports and control their sales operation pipelines.

- **Project Management Tools**: Project Management Tools hook up with Trello Asana or Jira to create automated systems for project tracking as well as team collaboration updates which results in smooth project management.

Project Management Tools

2. Data Syncing

- **Real-Time Data Access**: Microsoft 365 apps gain real-time data access because users can visualize analytics directly from third-party applications after an automatic data synchronization process.

- **Automatic Updates**: The system should monitor third-party application modifications to refresh Microsoft tool information and preserve the newest data available for decision-making.

3. Collaboration Enhancements

- **Unified Communication**: The Copilot service inside Microsoft Teams enables users to communicate with third-party messaging applications which supports business connections between internal staff and external partners or clients.
- **Shared Workspaces**: Microsoft users should build shared workspaces that combine Microsoft application resources alongside third-party application tools in order to support collaboration between different teams.

4. Custom Connectors

- **Power Automate Integration**: Users can utilize Microsoft Power Automate to establish customized workflows that automate procedures for connecting Microsoft 365 products with various third-party software systems.

- **API Access**: A payment approach combining APIs allows organizations to design customized connections specific to their business applications for improved functionality and data control.

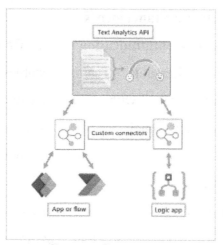

Custom Connectors

5. Enhanced Analytics

- **Business Intelligence Tools**: The integration of BI tools such as Tableau and Power BI allows businesses to retrieve external data sets which enable them to perform in-depth analysis with visualization capabilities for reporting within Microsoft applications.

- **Data Enrichment**: Existing data will become more accurate through third-party data enrichment that brings complementary information into the system.

Enhanced Analytics

6. Security and Compliance

- **Data Protection**: Data Protection can be achieved by making sure Microsoft security guidelines apply to third-party app connections which also protects data integrity and maintains regulatory compliance.
- **Access Controls**: The system must implement access control features to oversee and control rights for external integration access so sensitive data remains secure.

Summary

Microsoft Copilot becomes more functional when users can integrate it with third-party applications because it enables automatic workflow operations and helps users reach diverse data sets as well as work together on multiple platforms efficiently. The current work environment functions more cohesively because of these integrative capabilities which leads organizations toward their goal achievement and productivity improvement.

CHAPTER SIX

BEST PRACTICES

Tips for Effective Use of Microsoft Copilot

The following guidelines will help you extract the maximum advantages from Microsoft Copilot alongside increased productivity:

1. Familiarize Yourself with Features

- Devote several minutes on familiarizing yourself with different Microsoft 365 application features available within Copilot. A thorough knowledge of Copilot capabilities will lead to better usage of its potential.

2. Utilize Natural Language Queries

- Use Copilot to interpret instructions you type naturally. Tell Copilot what to do by asking basic commands like "Rephrase this document" and "Visualize sales statistics".

3. Customize Settings

- Rephrase Copilot's basic features according to your preferred choices. Set your preferences to manage notifications and task automation levels while adjusting writing settings to match your work system.

Customize Settings

4. Use Keyboard Shortcuts

- Learn all Microsoft applications keyboard shortcuts to work faster and smarter. Combining manual and Copilot-supported work tasks becomes easier when you use tools more rapidly.

5. Explore Templates

- Take advantage of built-in templates for document toolkits and slide designs from spreadsheets. You can tailor Copilot for document templates to suit your particular task requirements.

6. Integrate Third-Party Apps

- You can simplify workflow connections between Copilot and needed third-party applications. When integrated with third-party programs this helps you work with bigger datasets and control task schedules effectively.

Integrate Third-Party Apps

7. Take Advantage of Real-Time Collaboration

- Work efficiently with your colleagues in real time by accessing the collaboration function of Copilot within Teams and Word. Teams work better together when everyone uses Copilot to check their project alignment.

8. Review Suggestions Carefully

- When Copilot suggests something examine it before use to make sure the output matches both your content and requirements. Fit these changes to match your project needs.

9. Automate Repetitive Tasks

- Detect the tasks your team completes daily that Copilot can turn into automated processes. Allowing these processes to run using automated systems cuts down work hours and decreases potential mistakes.

10. Stay Updated

- Look for updates to Microsoft 365 and explore its new tool features regularly. The improvements made to Copilot regularly mean that following updates helps you gain maximum benefit from its features.

11. Provide Feedback

- Tell Microsoft what you think about Copilot's functioning and add-ons. Your feedback helps Microsoft improve both user features and the functionality of Copilot.

12. Leverage Help and Tutorials

- You should take advantage of Microsoft help tools to learn more about its Copilot functions. When you use built-in learning materials you will discover important methods and recommendations to use the tool better.

Summary

Using these suggestions will help you get more out of Microsoft Copilot while making your work processes faster and improving your production in Microsoft 365 tools. You can get better results from your work by using the full power of Copilot.

Common Use Cases for Microsoft Copilot

Microsoft Copilot delivers multiple tools that help users in many different fields with their tasks. The following situations feature Microsoft Copilot's widespread applications:

1. Document Drafting and Editing

- **Business Reports**: The tool assists our team with business reporting by applying data analysis to generate professional documents requiring no writing.
- **Meeting Notes**: Pattern Hidden written meeting notes point out what participants talked about and what tasks they agreed to handle.

2. Data Analysis and Visualization

- **Sales Performance Tracking**: Our AI system uses Excel to examine sales performance and builds visualization reports plus sales forecast predictions.
- **Financial Analysis**: The AI system Copilot helps you create financial models and prepares budgets plus reports that display essential financial information.

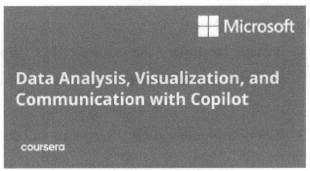

Data Analysis and Visualization

3. Project Management

- **Task Automation**: The system uses task automation in Microsoft Planner and Teams to speed up project workflow processes.
- **Progress Reporting**: The system creates simple progress reports that review project stages and work results for clear stakeholder updates.

Project Management

4. Email Management

- **Email Drafting**: The software lets you create multiple emails instantly alongside basic work replies and tracks all correspondence.

- **Email Summarization**: The system will distill long email correspondence to show only the important details so that users can handle their discussions better.

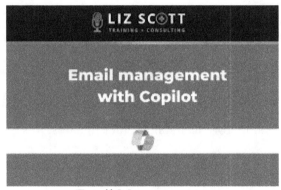

Email Management

5. Presentation Creation

- **Slide Deck Generation**: Use comments from Copilot to generate slides from documents and data and build better presentation content plans.

- **Content Enhancement**: Help players make better presentations by suggesting visual data formats and panel structure within their content.

6. Customer Relationship Management (CRM)

- **Lead Management**: Look at CRM system data to find lead activity levels and convert sales success.

- **Personalized Communication**: You can create custom emails or messages based on what users do and what they like to see.

7. Team Collaboration

- **Collaborative Document Editing**: Users can edit documents together with their team while Copilot supports their document creation work.

- **Feedback Integration**: The team can enhance their document editing process when they input feedback into documents and presentations.

Team Collaboration

8. Training and Onboarding

- **Training Material Creation**: Copilot quickly makes training assets through ready-to-use templates while its text-generation helps authors create output faster.

- **Onboarding Checklists**: Develop onboarding checklists and action plans to guide new hires on their first days and provide them all essential support.

9. Content Marketing

- **Blog Post Drafting**: Turn blog material drafts into reality by asking Copilot to suggest headlines and body content.

- **Social Media Content**: Use Microsoft Copilot to design effective social media content that targets our audience based on data analysis.

Summary

Microsoft Copilot helps different industries and tasks achieve better results through its general applications. Microsoft Copilot helps users accomplish all their tasks more effectively by improving data-based choices and enabling smoother communication.

CHAPTER SEVEN

TROUBLESHOOTING

Frequently Asked Questions (FAQs) about Microsoft Copilot

1. What is Microsoft Copilot?

Users get better productivity results through Microsoft 365 applications when they use Microsoft Copilot as their AI-powered writing and task-handling assistant.

2. Which Microsoft applications support Copilot?

You can find Copilot working in all major Microsoft 365 applications including Word, Excel, PowerPoint, Outlook, and Teams.

3. How does Copilot assist with writing?

Copilot delivers writing assistance by suggesting text instantly plus it produces content from input topics while checking grammar and document design.

4. Can I use Copilot for data analysis?

With Microsoft Excel Copilot users can process data analysis tasks like generating report snapshots and charts along with detecting patterns while running mathematical computations based on verbal instructions.

5. Is Copilot able to automate tasks?

Absolutely! Copilot enables users to have their meetings scheduled and reports generated automatically to free up their time while making operations run more smoothly.

6. How do I set up Copilot?

The Microsoft 365 plan is needed to enable Copilot service. After creating your account you can sign in to supported Microsoft 365 applications to access Copilot features.

7. Are there any system requirements for using Copilot?

To access and make the most of Copilot users need to have Microsoft 365 version support plus a working internet connection. Check Microsoft's website to find out its exact system requirements.

8. Can Copilot integrate with third-party applications?

Copilot enables users to link workflow automation tools and connect to Microsoft 365 data sources from multiple other applications.

9. Is my data secure while using Copilot?

The company puts security first by making sure Copilot handles enterprise-level data protection requirements and follows legal rules for confidential information.

10. How can I provide feedback on Copilot?

Users can leave feedback from inside the Microsoft 365 tools that support Copilot function. Find the built-in feedback option from within each application to tell Microsoft what you think.

Summary

This document handles questions from users about how Microsoft Copilot functions with its installation and security features. Users can find all necessary details about Copilot by reading the official Microsoft documents and support materials.

Common Issues and Solutions for Microsoft Copilot

These are the commonplace Microsoft Copilot issues taken after by conceivable answers:

1. Copilot Not Responding

- **Issue**: The Copilot instrument does not provide any reactions or shows up inert to commands.
- **Solution**: To settle this issue confirm that your web remains associated. Revive the app or detach your Microsoft 365 account and reenter it. When the issue proceeds you ought to expel the put away information or introduce the application once more.

2. Inaccurate Suggestions

- **Issue**: When Copilot proposes inaccurate or dishonorable arrangements it gets to be a issue.
- **Solution**: Offer assistance Copilot work superior by giving it exact enlightening in each ask. When proposals stay erroneous you ought to utilize the criticism framework to report them since clients offer assistance create the show.

3. Integration Problems with Third-Party Apps

- **Issue**: It is challenging to interface information appropriately between third-party programs and Microsoft 365.

- **Solution**: Check in the event that your third-party app interfaces with Microsoft 365 administrations and affirm it has the required authorizations. See through API controls and make beyond any doubt all program programs have later overhauls.

4. Performance Slowdowns

- **Issue**: The application runs moderate once you empower Copilot highlights.

- **Solution**: Near extra open programs and browser windows to boost execution. Test your gadget against Copilot framework needs and supplant ancient equipment when it benefits execution.

5. Copilot Not Available in Some Regions

- **Issue**: Clients who need to utilize Copilot highlights find the benefit isn't given in their particular area.

- **Solution**: To check in case Copilot highlights are accessible visit Microsoft's official site and discover your locale points of interest. Microsoft overhauls

Copilot features in stages which suggests the device might not as of now be available all over.

6. Data Privacy Concerns

- **Issue**: Numerous clients stress as they need to know how Microsoft Copilot ensures their individual information.

- **Solution**: Look at how Microsoft secures your individual data in its approaches and security settings. Upgrade to the foremost later adaptation of Microsoft 365 to induce the current security improvements.

Data Privacy Concerns

7. Issues with Document Formatting

- **Issue**: The formatting options that Copilot suggests do not stick properly.

- **Solution**: Review the recommendations for changes to make carefully when reviewing them. After Copilot applies changes you can easily make formatting adjustments by hand.

8. Difficulty Accessing Help Resources

- **Issue**: The system does not provide enough instructions and help materials for Copilot.
- **Solution**: Go to Microsoft support through its web platform or use the built-in help system inside the applications. Community forums offer users special knowledge that you can access for better Copilot usage.

9. Copilot Crashing or Freezing

- **Issue**: Copilot stops working regularly when it needs to perform its task.
- **Solution**: Keep your software up to date at all times. Test various software and extensions until you find one that triggers the crashing problem.

Copilot Crashing or Freezing

10. Limited Functionality in Offline Mode

- **Issue**: The Copilot system has few functions available without internet connection.

- **Solution**: Stick to a reliable internet connection for Copilot to work as expected. Look for built-in offline features in the product.

Summary

Users can improve their Copilot experience through these proposed solutions while fixing typical Microsoft products' issues. When regular solutions fail you should reach out to Microsoft's official support network for further help.

CHAPTER EIGHT

APPENDIX

Glossary of Terms for Microsoft Copilot

These terms define Microsoft Copilot and what it can do:

1. AI (Artificial Intelligence)

A system processes human-like data to think like humans while also handling spoken commands and performing data calculations.

2. Automation

Technology algorithms perform tasks without manual support based on preset procedures.

3. Collaboration

Group members use collaboration tools to add their work at the same time to create group outcomes.

4. CRM (Customer Relationship Management)

An application that helps businesses in overseeing communications with clients for way better relationship building and exchange development.

5. Data Visualization

A strategy appears information outwardly to bolster clients get it complicated data through picture-based shows.

6. Dashboard

A show framework that puts basic execution pointers and visual shows forthright for easy perusing.

7. Integration

An approach to connect different computer programs and frameworks so they work together fluidly without intrusions.

8. Document Formatting

A archive framework employments content format methods additionally plan components to make way better data shows and visual offer.

Document Formatting

9. Natural Language Processing (NLP)

AI department examining how computers prepare and answer to human communications in standard discourse.

Natural Language Processing (NLP)

10. Prompt

You provide Copilot verbal enlightening to start performing assignments or making substance that you just need.

11. Reporting

Information organization into a characterized format makes a difference individuals take superior choices and think about comes about.

12. Task Automation

Technology performs work schedules naturally to move forward quicker preparing of assignments.

13. Template

You'll utilize pre-made archive and format layouts to construct unused work successfully and keep up consistency.

14. Version Control

Clients can utilize this framework to screen their record alters and go back to past adaptations when required.

15. Workflow

Work goes through requested work steps that get mechanized to extend proficiency and diminish client labor.

Summary

This list clarifies essential Microsoft Copilot terms and their related highlights to assist clients comprehend the apparatus way better. Information of these terms makes strides how clients associated with Microsoft Copilot and its suite of items.

Update History for Microsoft Copilot

This area presents the most discharges of Microsoft Copilot through forms:

Version 1.0 (Initial Release)

- **Launch Date**: [Insert Launch Date]
- **Features**:
  - Essential composing help in Word and Viewpoint.
  - Introductory information examination capabilities in Exceed expectations.
  - Assignment computerization functionalities presented.

Version 1.1 (Feature Enhancements)

- **Release Date**: [Insert Release Date]
- **Updates**:
  - The framework presently gets it characteristic dialect way better by preparing writings in full settings.

- Exceed expectations incorporates additional ways to appear information through unused chart alternatives.
- Starting integration with third-party applications.

Version 1.2 (Collaboration Tools)

- **Release Date**: [Insert Release Date]
- **Updates**:
  - Partners and Word clients can alter PDFs together in genuine time.
  - Improved assembly summarization capabilities in Groups.
  - Our framework now provides superior ways to get record input amid altering.

Version 2.0 (Major Update)

- **Release Date**: [Insert Release Date]
- **Updates**:
  - Noteworthy headways in AI calculations for more exact recommendations.
  - Extended bolster for venture administration tools and CRM integrative.
  - Presentation of customizable layouts for archives and introductions.

Version 2.1 (User Experience Improvements)

- **Release Date**: [Insert Release Date]
- **Updates**:
    - Our unused framework empowers superior client get to through an moved forward visual plan framework.
    - Presentation of modern preparing assets and instructional exercises inside the app.
    - Progressed execution and speed upgrades over all applications.

Version 2.2 (Security and Compliance)

- **Release Date**: [Insert Release Date]
- **Updates**:
    - The upgrades contained more grounded security strategies to guard client protection and individual information.
    - Our item needs security and industry directions upgrades to coordinate current needs.
    - Clients get to control how their individual information is transmitted to other clients in this overhaul.

Version 3.0 (Expanded Capabilities)

- **Release Date**: [Insert Release Date]
- **Updates**:
  - Major upgrades in prescient analytics and machine learning capabilities.
  - The item will presently interface to distinctive outside apps and administrations.
  - The upgrade brings effective unused capacities to oversee commerce substance in PowerPoint slides.

Summary

This document shows how Microsoft Copilot received new features and updates throughout its history. Users should visit Microsoft's official website to access the most recent release notes and product documentation about Microsoft Copilot.

CHAPTER NINE

FEEDBACK

How to Provide Feedback on Microsoft Copilot

The Microsoft Copilot needs user feedback for product teams to develop superior features alongside interface improvements. Going through these steps enables you to send Microsoft Copilot feedback:

1. In-App Feedback Option

- **Accessing Feedback**: Users can access the features for providing feedback which most Microsoft 365 tools integrate within their platforms. The feedback tool exists in the Help section together with the app Settings area.

- **Submitting Feedback**: To help Microsoft enhance the product users can navigate to Feedback through the app menu to eventually finish and deliver the feedback form. Give complete details about good experiences together with all difficulties you encountered.

2. Microsoft Feedback Portal

- **Visit the Portal**: Users can reach the Microsoft Feedback Portal through its online interface in order to make product suggestions or document technical issues.

- **Create an Account**: The first step to provide feedback requires Microsoft account sign-up processes after establishing a Microsoft account.
- **Browse Existing Feedback**: Check for Feedback that Already Exists by Scanning Through What Previous Users Have Submitted. By voting on your computer you add support to existing suggestions that exist within the system.

3. Community Forums

- **Join the Microsoft Community**: Users need to become a member of the Microsoft Community to participate in Microsoft Tech Community discussions about their Microsoft product usage.
- **Post Your Feedback**: Post Your Feedback allows you to inform others about Copilot by starting dialogues that attract Microsoft community member feedback.

4. Customer Support

- **Contact Support**: Major difficulties with Copilot features enable users to reach Microsoft Support directly through their contact channels. You can identify all contact channels through the Microsoft Support site.

- **Provide Details**: Contact us with complete details of your issue including a step-by-step guidance that allows problem duplication and visual evidence.

Customer Support

5. Social Media Channels

- **Engage on Social Media**: Follow Microsoft through Twitter and LinkedIn along with Facebook to join their online social presence. Reach out to Microsoft directly through tagging of their official social pages.

- **Use Hashtags**: Use appropriate hashtags which include #Microsoft365 and #CopilotFeedback to improve the visibility of your feedback.

Summary

Through these channels you can effectively convey Microsoft Copilot feedback to Microsoft so that the tool can grow better along with its experience capabilities. Your feedback keeps the development of new Copilot features progressing forward for an ongoing improvement cycle.

Community Forums for Microsoft Copilot

The community forum gives users multiple opportunities to exchange experiences and obtain support and give feedback for Microsoft Copilot. You can find three important community forums for active participation. These include:

1. Microsoft Tech Community

- **Overview**: Microsoft Tech Community operates as a specific platform for all Microsoft users to share product knowledge while seeking assistance through both expert and peer support.
- **Access**: Microsoft Tech Community
- **Features**:
  - o The Microsoft 365 tools and Copilot form part of the topic-specific discussions available on these community platforms.

o Within these forums users can pose inquiries along with giving input that leads to resolving routine problems.

2. Microsoft Answers

- **Overview**: Users can ask questions through Microsoft Answers who receive responses either from community members or Microsoft support staff.
- **Access**: <u>Microsoft Answers</u>
- **Features**:
  o The database contains a searchable collection of questions together with their corresponding answers.
  o Users can submit fresh questions concerning Copilot together with other Microsoft products through this feature.

3. Stack Overflow

- **Overview**: The programming platform Stack Overflow welcomes developers and technical users who post and answer questions about Microsoft products among others.
- **Access**: <u>Stack Overflow</u>
-

- **Features**:
  - o The site answers both development-related and practical questions about integrating Copilot in development processes through a question-and-answer system.
  - o Community-driven support with a vast pool of knowledgeable users.

Stack Overflow

4. Reddit

- **Overview**: Reddit hosts multiple subreddits regarding Microsoft products that enable users to exchange information about product features together with helpful tips and feedback opportunities.
- **Access**: Examples include:
  - o r/Microsoft365
  - o r/Office365

- **Features**:
  - ○ Informal discussions and user experiences.
  - ○ The user can participate in discussions about Copilot while also having the chance to pose queries and offer their professional insights regarding the tool.

5. LinkedIn Groups

- **Overview**: The LinkedIn platform provides professional user-focused groups which concentrate on Microsoft technology development and user platform experiences.
- **Access**: You can find Microsoft 365 and Copilot related groups through searching on LinkedIn.
- **Features**:
  - ○ Networking with professionals in your field.
  - ○ These groups share Microsoft tool best practices together with practical tips and obtain feedback on Microsoft system usage.

Summary

These open community platforms allow users to build network connections through insight sharing that provides valuable information about Microsoft Copilot. The community provides an opportunity to deepen your knowledge of the tool while creating an environment for your suggestions to be assessed.

www.ingramcontent.com/pod-product-compliance
Lightning Source LLC
Chambersburg PA
CBHW071009050326
40689CB00014B/3551